Directory of National Programs

Federal Bureau of Prisons

INTRODUCTION

Supporting a successful transition to the community is central to the mission of the Federal Bureau of Prisons (Bureau). The Bureau protects public safety by ensuring that federal inmates receive reentry programming to support their successful return to the community. National programs are the Bureau's premier reentry programs, designed to ensure that inmates have the skills necessary to succeed upon release. National programs are standardized across institutions, described in the Bureau's national policies, implemented with dedicated resources, and regularly reviewed for quality assurance. When appropriate, national programs are developed or modified to address the needs of specific populations within the Bureau. For example, a gender-responsive version of the Residential Drug Abuse Treatment Program has been created to specifically address the treatment needs of female inmates.

This practical guide was prepared to highlight the Bureau's national programs. Each program summary in this directory contains key information: a Program Description, Time Frame, Admission Criteria, Program Content, Empirical Support, Applicable Policies, and Institution Locations. Additional information about these programs can be obtained by accessing the referenced policies, which are available on the Bureau's public website: www.bop.gov. More specific inquiries about these programs should be directed to the responsible disciplines with the Bureau, as identified in the Table of Contents.

In addition to national programs, the Bureau maintains a catalog of evidence-based and promising model programs to address a wide range of reentry needs. Programs contained in this catalog are implemented at the local level with existing resources. These supplemental program offerings vary based on available resources and the needs of each institution's inmate population. Each institution's Reentry Affairs Coordinator maintains a list of the model programs that is currently available at his/her institution.

Disclaimer: The Bureau provides this directory as a means of describing programs offered throughout the agency. This list contains information which is accurate as of November 2016, but programming offered at various institutions is subject to change over time. The Bureau attempts to follow all judicial recommendations regarding place of incarceration; however, many factors are considered when making a designation decision and the Bureau is not always able to accommodate a judicial recommendation.

Table of Contents

Bureau Literacy Program

Program Description	The Literacy Program is designed to help inmates develop foundational knowledge and skill in reading, math, and written expression, and to prepare inmates to get a General Educational Development (GED) credential. Completion of the Literacy Program is often only the first step towards adequate preparation for successful post-release reintegration into society.
Time Frame	Depending on student needs, students participate in literacy classes for a varied length of time. Literacy classes are scheduled Monday through Friday. Each literacy class session meets a minimum of 1 1/2 hours per day. With few exceptions, inmates without a confirmed GED or high school diploma are required to enroll and participate in the Literacy Program for a minimum of 240 instructional hours or until they achieve a GED credential.
Admission Criteria	All inmates without a GED credential or a high school diploma are enrolled in literacy classes in Bureau correctional facilities. The following inmates are not required to attend the Literacy Program; (1) pretrial inmates; (2) inmates committed for purpose of study and observation under the provisions of 18 U.S.C. 4205(c), 4241(d), or, effective November 1, 1987, 18 U.S.C. 3552(b); (3) sentenced deportable aliens; and (4) inmates determined by staff to be temporarily unable to participate in the Literacy Program due to special circumstances beyond their control (e.g., due to a medical condition, transfer on writ, on a waiting list for initial placement). However, these inmates are required to participate when the special circumstances are no longer applicable.
Program Content	Program content focuses on developing foundational knowledge and skill in reading, math, and written expression, and to prepare inmates to get a GED credential. Inmates withdrawing from literacy programs prior to obtaining a GED will be restricted to the lowest pay and have an inability to vest or earn the maximum amount of Good Conduct Time. Occupational training programs generally require a GED/High School Diploma or concurrent enrollment in a Literacy Program.
Empirical Support	Research has shown that passing the GED Test increases earnings for some dropouts, but labor market payoffs take time (Murnane, Willett, & Tyler, 2000; Tyler, 2004; Tyler & Berk, 2008; Tyler, Murnane, & Willett, 2000, 2003). GED credentials provide a pathway into postsecondary education, and finishing even a short term program offers important economic benefits to GED credential recipients (Patterson, Zhang, Song & Guison-Dowdy, 2010).
Applicable Policies	5350.28 Literacy Program (GED Standard) 5300.21 Education Training and Leisure Time Program Standards 5353.01 Occupational Education Programs
Institution Locations	All Bureau facilities offer the Literacy Program.

English-as-a-Second Language Program

Program Description	The English-as-a-Second Language (ESL) Program is designed to help limited English proficient inmates improve their English until they function at the equivalency of the eighth grade level in listening and reading comprehension.
Time Frame	Depending on English skills and motivation, inmates participate in the ESL program for a varied length of time. ESL classes are scheduled Monday through Friday. Each class session meets a minimum of 1 ½ hours per day. With few exceptions, limited English proficient inmates are required to participate in the ESL program until they function at the eighth grade level as measured by standardized reading and listening assessment tests.
Admission Criteria	All limited English proficient inmates in the Bureau's correctional facilities are required to participate in the ESL Program. The following inmates are exempt from the mandatory ESL participation requirement: (1) pretrial inmates; (2) inmates committed for the purpose of study and observation under the provisions of 18 U.S.C. 4205(c) or, effective November 1, 1987, 18 U.S.C. 3552 (b); (3) sentenced aliens with a deportation detainer; and (4) other inmates whom, for documented good cause, the Warden may excuse from attending the ESL program. Such inmates, however, shall be required to participate when the special circumstances are no longer applicable. Although exempted from mandatory ESL participation requirement, all limited proficient English speaking inmates are strongly encouraged to participate in the ESL Program.
Program Content	Program content primarily focuses on developing functional English listening and reading comprehension skills such as locating and utilizing resources (e.g., libraries, public transportation, drug stores, grocery stores, employment opportunities).
Empirical Support	Research has shown that individuals who are literate only in a language other than English are more likely to have non-continuous employment and earn less than those literate in English (Greenberg, Macas, Rhodes, & Chan, 2001). Data from the 2000 U.S. Census on immigrant earnings revealed a positive relation between earnings and English skill ability (Chiswick & Miller, 2002). An analysis of higher quality research studies has shown, on average, inmates who participated in correctional education programs (to include ESL instruction) had a 43% lower recidivism rate than those inmates who did not participate (Davis et al., 2014). The same research study also demonstrated correctional education is cost effective (i.e., a savings of $5 on re-incarceration costs for every $1 spent on correctional education).
Applicable Policies	5300.21 Education Training and Leisure Time Program Standards 5350.24 English-as-a-Second Language Program (ESL)
Institution Locations	All Bureau facilities offer the ESL Program.

Federal Prison Industries Program

Program Description	The mission of Federal Prison Industries, (FPI) Inc. is to protect society and reduce crime by preparing inmates for successful reentry through job training. FPI (also known by its trade name UNICOR) is a critical component of the Bureau's comprehensive efforts to improve inmate reentry. By providing inmates the skills needed to join the workforce upon release, FPI reduces recidivism and helps curb the rising costs of corrections. FPI was established in 1934 by statute and executive order to provide opportunities for training and work experience to federal inmates (18 U.S.C. § 4121, et seq.). FPI does not rely on tax dollars for support; its operations are completely self-sustaining. FPI is overseen by a Presidentially-appointed Board of Directors. It is one of the Bureau's most critical programs in support of reentry and recidivism reduction.
Time Frame	Employment opportunities are dependent upon institutional needs, FPI requirements, and the inmate employment waiting list.
Admission Criteria	Inmate workers are ordinarily hired through waiting lists. A renewed emphasis has been placed on the use of job share and half-time workers. This will allow for an increase in the number of inmates who benefit from participating in the FPI program. FPI has placed emphasis on prioritizing inmates on the waiting list within two years of release for available FPI positions, with the aim these inmates should be hired at least six months prior to release. FPI has also placed an emphasis on prioritizing inmates on the waiting list who are military veterans, as well as those with financial responsibilities.
Program Content	FPI is, first and foremost, a correctional program. Its impetus is helping inmates acquire the skills necessary to successfully make the transition from prison to law-abiding, tax paying, productive members of society. The production of items and provision of services are necessary by-products of those efforts, as FPI does not receive any appropriated funds for operation.
Empirical Support	Rigorous research, as outlined in the Post-Release Employment Project (PREP Study), demonstrates participation in prison industries and vocational training programs has a positive effect on post-release employment and recidivism. The research revealed inmates who worked in prison industries were 24% less likely to recidivate than non-program participants and 14% more likely to be gainfully employed. These programs had an even greater positive impact on minority inmates who are at a greater risk of recidivism.
Applicable Policies	8120.02 Work Programs for Inmates – FPI 1600.10 Environmental Management Systems 5180.05 Central Inmate Monitoring System 5251.06 Work and Performance Pay Program, Inmate 5290.14 Admission and Orientation Program 5353.01 Occupational Education Programs 5350.28 Literacy Program (GED Standard) 5380.08 Financial Responsibility Program, Inmate 8000.01 UNICOR Corporate Policy and Procedures
	The Federal Prison Industries Program is available at the following facilities:

Institution Locations	Mid-Atlantic Region	North Central Region	Northeast Region
	FCI Ashland, KY-Low FCI Beckley, WV-Medium FCC Butner, NC-Complex FCI Cumberland, MD-Medium FCI Gilmer, WV-Medium FMC Lexington, KY-Adm. FCI Manchester, KY-Medium FCI Memphis, TN-Medium FCC Petersburg, VA-Complex	FCI Englewood, CO-Low FCI Greenville, IL-Medium USP Leavenworth, KS-Medium USP Marion, IL-Medium FCI Milan, MI-Low FCI Sandstone, MN-Low FCC Terre Haute, IN-Complex FCI Waseca, MN-Low (F)	FCC Allenwood, PA-Complex FCI Elkton, OH-Low FCI Fairton, NJ-Medium FCI Fort Dix, NJ-Low USP Lewisburg, PA-High FCI Schuylkill, PA-Medium
	South Central Region	Southeast Region	Western Region
	FCI Bastrop, TX-Low FCC Beaumont, TX-Complex FPC Bryan, TX-Minimum (F) FCI El Reno, OK-Medium FCC Forrest City, AR-Complex FCI La Tuna, TX-Low FCC Oakdale, LA- Complex FCC Pollock, LA- Complex FCI Seagoville, TX-Low FCI Texarkana, TX-Low	USP Atlanta, GA-Medium FCC Coleman, FL-Complex FCI Edgefield, SC-Medium FCI Jesup, GA-Medium FCI Marianna, FL-Medium FCI Miami, FL-Low FPC Montgomery, AL-Minimum FPC Pensacola, FL-Minimum FCI Talladega, AL- Medium FCI Tallahassee, FL-Low (F) FCC Yazoo City, MS-Complex	USP Atwater, CA-High FCI Dublin, CA-Low (F) FCC Lompoc, CA-Complex FCI Phoenix, AZ-Medium FCI Safford, AZ-Low FCI Sheridan, OR-Medium FCI Terminal Island, CA - Low FCC Tucson, AZ-Complex FCC Victorville, CA-Complex
	(F) = Female Program		

Occupational Education Programs

Program Description	The Occupational Education Program is designed to help inmates acquire marketable skills in a wide variety of trades. Programs which vary from institution to institution are provided by either career civil-service vocational training instructors or through contracts with colleges and technical schools. Many institutions also provide registered apprenticeships through the United States Department of Labor's Office of Apprenticeship. The current Inmate Occupational Training Directory, outlining the specifics for programs offered at each institution is accessible via: http://www.bop.gov/inmates/custody_and_care/docs/inmate_occupational_training_directory.pdf
Time Frame	Program length varies with the provider and the complexity of the program. Upon completion of a marketable occupational education program, inmates may earn an AA, AS, AAS degree and/or an industry recognized certification. Apprenticeship programs are usually 2,000+ hours and may take three to four years to complete.
Admission Criteria	All inmates are eligible to participate in an institution's occupational education program. The inmate's unit team, in consultation with the Education Department, determines if a particular course of study is suited to the inmate's needs. Occupational education programs typically require an inmate to have a GED or high school diploma or concurrent enrollment in the Literacy Program. Inmates under orders of deportation, exclusion, or removal may participate in an institution's occupational education program if institution resources permit after meeting the needs of other eligible inmates.
Program Content	Program content focuses on developing the skills necessary for entry-level employment in a given trade.
Empirical Support	Evidence shows a relationship between correctional education program participation before release and lower odds of recidivating after release (Davis et al., 2014; Saylor and Gaes, 1996; Aos, Phipps, Barnoski and Lieb, 2001). In a study conducted in Maryland, Minnesota and Ohio, correctional education participants had lower recidivism rates in the categories of re-arrest, re-conviction, and re-incarceration (Steurer, Smith and Tracy, 2001). There is some evidence that in-prison vocational education is effective in improving the likelihood of post-release employment (Davis et al., 2014).
Applicable Policies	5353.01 Occupational Education Programs 5300.21 Education, Training and Leisure Time Program Standards
Institution Locations	All Bureau facilities are mandated to offer Occupational Training with the following exceptions: metropolitan correctional centers, metropolitan/federal detention centers, the Federal Transfer Center, satellite camps, and the administrative maximum facility.

Parenting Program

Program Description	The Parenting Program provides inmates information and counseling through directed classes on how to enhance their relationship with their children even while incarcerated. All parenting programs include a classroom component and relationship building visitation activities. In addition, social services outreach contacts are often established to facilitate the provision of services to the inmate parent, visiting custodial parent, and children.
Time Frame	Inmates may participate in the Parenting Program at any point during their sentence. The duration of the program varies by institution-to-institution.
Admission Criteria	All inmates are afforded the opportunity to participate in the Parenting Program.
Program Content	The Parenting Program varies in length, depth, and content from institution-to-institution. Providers of Parenting Program components may include educational staff, as well as volunteers from a community group and/or a social service organization. However, the program's curriculum is recommended to address parenting skills, skills for family support, family literacy education, substance abuse education, and prenatal care information for expectant mothers. Content may be supplemented by curriculum contained in the Model Programs Catalog.
Empirical Support	Research has shown parenting programs for incarcerated parents can improve their self-esteem, parenting attitudes, and institutional adjustment.
Applicable Policies	5355.03 Parenting Program Standards 5267.09 Visiting Regulations 5300.20 Volunteer Services 5300.21 Education Training and Leisure Time Program Standards
Institution Locations	All Bureau facilities offer the Parenting Program.

Bureau Rehabilitation and Values Enhancement Program

Program Description	The Bureau Rehabilitation and Values Enhancement (BRAVE) Program is a cognitive-behavioral, residential treatment program for young males, serving their first federal sentence. Programming is delivered within a modified therapeutic community environment; inmates participate in interactive groups and attend community meetings. The BRAVE Program is designed to facilitate favorable institutional adjustment and reduce incidents of misconduct. In addition, the program encourages inmates to interact positively with staff members and take advantage of opportunities to engage in self-improvement activities throughout their incarceration.
Time Frame	The BRAVE Program is a six-month program. Inmates participate in treatment groups for four hours per day, Monday through Friday. As the BRAVE Program is designed to facilitate a favorable initial adjustment to incarceration, inmates are assigned to the program at the beginning of their sentence.
Admission Criteria	Program admission criteria are as follows: medium security male inmate, 32 years of age or younger, a sentence of 60 months or more, and new to the federal system.
Program Content	Program content focuses on developing interpersonal skills, behaving pro-socially in a prison environment, challenging antisocial attitudes and criminality, developing problem solving skills, and planning for release.
Empirical Support	Research found BRAVE Program participants had a misconduct rate lower than a comparison group and BRAVE Program graduates also had a lower misconduct rate. The BRAVE Program utilizes cognitive behavioral treatment within a modified therapeutic community; these interventions have been found to be effective with an incarcerated population in the reduction of recidivism.
Applicable Policies	5330.11 CN-1 Psychology Treatment Programs
Institution Locations	The BRAVE Program is located at the following facilities: FCI Beckley, WV-Medium FCI Victorville, CA-Medium

Challenge Program

Program Description	The Challenge Program is a cognitive-behavioral, residential treatment program developed for male inmates in penitentiary settings. The Challenge Program provides treatment to high security inmates with substance abuse problems and/or mental illnesses. Programming is delivered within a modified therapeutic community environment; inmates participate in interactive groups and attend community meetings. In addition to treating substance use disorders and mental illnesses, the program addresses criminality, via cognitive-behavioral challenges to criminal thinking errors. The Challenge Program is available in most high security institutions.
Time Frame	Inmates may participate in the program at any point during their sentence; however, they must have at least 18 months remaining on their sentence. The duration of the program varies based on inmate need, with a minimum duration of nine months.
Admission Criteria	A high security inmate must meet one of the following criteria to be eligible to participate in the Challenge Program: a history of substance abuse/dependence or a major mental illness as evidenced by a current diagnosis of a psychotic disorder, mood disorder, anxiety disorder, or personality disorder.
Program Content	The Challenge Program focuses on the reduction of antisocial peer associations; promotion of positive relationships; increased self-control and problem solving skills; and development of pro-social behaviors. The program places a special emphasis on violence prevention. In addition, there are separate supplemental protocols for inmates with substance use disorders and inmates with serious mental illnesses.
Empirical Support	Interventions used in the Challenge Program (i.e., cognitive-behavioral protocols and a modified therapeutic community model) have been demonstrated to be effective in other treatment programs, such as the Bureau's Residential Drug Abuse Program and BRAVE Program. Specifically, they have been noted to reduce misconduct, substance abuse/dependence, and recidivism. The mental health interventions selected for the Challenge Program also have strong empirical support and appear in multiple evidence-based programs (EBPs) registries.
Applicable Policies	5330.11 CN-1 Psychology Treatment Programs

Institution Locations

The Challenge Program is available at the following facilities:

Mid-Atlantic Region	North Central Region	Northeast Region
USP Big Sandy, KY-High USP Hazelton, WV-High USP Lee, VA-High USP McCreary, KY-High	USP Terre Haute, IN-High	USP Allenwood, PA-High USP Canaan, PA-High

Southeast Region	South Central Region	Western Region
USP Coleman I, FL-High USP Coleman II, FL-High	USP Beaumont, TX-High USP Pollock, LA-High	USP Atwater, CA-High USP Tucson, AZ-High

Drug Abuse Education

Program Description	Drug Abuse Education is designed to encourage inmates with a history of drug use to review the consequences of their choice to use drugs and the physical, social, and psychological impacts of this choice. Drug Abuse Education is designed to motivate appropriate inmates to participate in drug abuse treatment, as needed; Drug Abuse Education is not drug treatment.
Time Frame	Drug Abuse Education is a 12-15 hour educational course. Class lengths and times are varied to meet the scheduling needs of each institution. Since the goal of Drug Abuse Education is to motivate inmates to participate in treatment, they are given the opportunity to participate in the course at the beginning of their sentence, ordinarily within the first 12 months.
Admission Criteria	Inmates are required to participate in Drug Abuse Education if any of the following criteria are met: their substance use contributed to the instant offense; their substance use resulted in a supervised release violation; a significant substance use history is noted; or a judicial recommendation for substance abuse treatment is noted. Additionally, any inmate may volunteer to take the course.
Program Content	Participants in Drug Abuse Education receive information on what distinguishes drug use, abuse, and addiction. Participants in the course also review their individual drug use histories, explore evidence of the nexus between drug use and crime, and identify negative consequences of continued drug abuse.
Empirical Support	Research has demonstrated psycho-educational techniques are effective motivational strategies, particularly in moving individuals toward seriously considering a significant life change.
Applicable Policies	5330.11 CN-1 Psychology Treatment Programs
Institution Locations	All Bureau facilities offer the Drug Abuse Education Program.

Mental Health Step Down Unit Program

Program Description	The Mental Health Step Down Unit Program is a residential treatment program offering an intermediate level of care for inmates with serious mental illnesses. The program is specifically designed to serve inmates who do not require inpatient treatment, but lack the skills to function in a general population prison setting. The program uses an integrative model that includes an emphasis on a modified therapeutic community, cognitive-behavioral therapies, and skills training. The goal of the Mental Health Step Down Unit Program is to provide evidence-based treatment to seriously mentally ill inmates in order to maximize their ability to function and minimize relapse and the need for inpatient hospitalization.
Time Frame	The Mental Health Step Down Unit Program is typically conducted over 12-18 months. Inmates may participate in the program at any point in their sentence. Formal programming is facilitated half-days, five days a week with the remaining half-day dedicated to an institution work assignment or other programming, as participants are able.
Admission Criteria	Inmates with serious mental illnesses, who would benefit from intensive residential treatment, are considered for the program. Inmates with a primary diagnosis of Borderline Personality Disorder are referred to the STAGES Program, as opposed to the Mental Health Step Down Unit Program. Program participants must volunteer for the program and must not be acutely mentally ill (i.e., they must not meet criteria for inpatient mental health treatment).
Program Content	Mental Health Step Down Unit Programs operate as modified therapeutic communities and utilize cognitive-behavioral treatments, cognitive rehabilitation, and skills training. Criminal thinking is addressed through the identification of criminal thinking errors and engagement in pro-social interactions with staff and peers. The programs work closely with Psychiatry Services to ensure participants receive appropriate medication and have the opportunity to build a positive relationship with the treating psychiatrist. Program content is designed to promote successful reentry into society at the conclusion of their term of incarceration, and program staff collaborate with community partners to facilitate reentry.
Empirical Support	The mental health interventions selected for this program have strong empirical support and appear in multiple evidence-based programs (EBPs) registries.
Applicable Policies	5330.11 CN-1 Psychology Treatment Programs
Institution Locations	Mental Health Step Down Unit Programs are available at the following facilities: USP Allenwood, PA-High (Secure) USP Atlanta, GA-Medium (Secure) FCI Butner, NC-Medium

Nonresidential Drug Abuse Program

Program Description	The Nonresidential Drug Abuse Program is a flexible, moderate intensity cognitive-behavioral treatment program. The program is designed to meet the needs of a variety of inmates including inmates who are waiting to enter the Residential Drug Abuse Program (RDAP); inmates who do not meet admission criteria for the RDAP, but who wish to benefit from less intensive drug abuse treatment services; and inmates who have been referred by other Psychology Services or institution staff for drug abuse treatment.
Time Frame	The Nonresidential Drug Abuse Program is comprised of 90-120 minute weekly group treatment sessions, for a minimum of 12 weeks and a maximum of 24 weeks. Treatment staff may offer treatment beyond the 12 week minimum based upon the treatment needs of the inmate and supplemental treatment services available at the facility.
Admission Criteria	An inmate must have a history of drug abuse as evidenced by self-report, Presentence Investigation Report (PSR) documentation, or incident reports for use of alcohol or drugs to be eligible to participate in the program.
Program Content	The Bureau's treatment of substance abuse includes a variety of clinical activities organized to treat complex psychological and behavioral problems. The activities are unified through the use of Cognitive Behavioral Therapy (CBT), which was selected as the theoretical model because of its proven effectiveness with the inmate population.
Empirical Support	The Nonresidential Drug Abuse Program utilizes cognitive-behavioral interventions, which have been proven to be effective in the treatment of substance use disorders. The group treatment format used in this program also offers empirically supported benefits from pro-social peer interaction among participants.
Applicable Policies	5330.11 CN-1 Psychology Treatment Programs
Institution Locations	All Bureau facilities offer the Nonresidential Drug Abuse Program.

Residential Drug Abuse Program

Program Description	The Residential Drug Abuse Program (RDAP) provides intensive cognitive-behavioral, residential drug abuse treatment. Programming is delivered within a modified therapeutic community environment; inmates participate in interactive groups and attend community meetings. The RDAP is currently available to Spanish speaking inmates at two facilities. In addition, Dual Diagnosis RDAPs provide specialized treatment services for the inmate with co-occurring substance abuse and mental illness and/or medical problems. Inmates who successfully complete the RDAP and meet other criteria (e.g., sufficient time remaining on their sentence, no precluding offense convictions) may be eligible for up to a 12 month sentence reduction.
Time Frame	The RDAP consists of a minimum of 500 hours of treatment programming delivered over the course of 9 to 12 months. In order to facilitate a successful transition to the community, most inmates participating in the RDAP have between 22 and 42 months remaining on their sentence when they begin the program.
Admission Criteria	In order to gain admission to the RDAP an inmate must meet all of the following admission criteria: US citizen; the presence of a verifiable substance use disorder within the 12 months prior to their arrest for the instant offense(s); able to participate in all three phases of the program, including transitional treatment in the Residential Reentry Center/home confinement; and a signed agreement acknowledging program responsibility.
Program Content	Program content focuses on reducing the likelihood of substance abuse through cognitive-behavioral interventions and relapse prevention strategies. The program also focuses on challenging antisocial attitudes and criminality. In addition, the program facilitates the development of interpersonal skills and pro-social behavior.
Empirical Support	In coordination with the National Institute on Drug Abuse (NIDA), the Bureau conducted a rigorous three-year outcome study of the RDAP, which was published in 2000. The study revealed that male participants were 16% less likely to recidivate and 15% less likely to relapse than similarly situated inmates who do not participate in residential drug abuse treatment for up to 3 years after release. The analysis also found that female inmates who participate in RDAP are 18% less likely to recidivate than similarly situated female inmates who do not participate in treatment.
Applicable Policies	5330.11 CN-1 Psychology Treatment Programs 5331.02 CN-1 Early Release Procedures Under U.S.C. 3621(e)

Institution Locations	The RDAP is available at the following facilities:		
	Mid-Atlantic Region	**North Central Region**	**Northeast Region**
	FPC Alderson, WV-Minimum (2, F) FCI Beckley, WV-Medium SCP Beckley, WV-Minimum USP Big Sandy, KY-High FCI Butner, NC-Medium (2) FCI Cumberland, MD-Medium SCP Cumberland, MD-Minimum SFF Hazelton, WV-Low (F) FMC Lexington, KY-Low FMC Lexington, KY-Low (D) FCI Memphis, TN-Medium FCI Morgantown, WV-Minimum (2) FCI Petersburg, VA-Low FCI Petersburg, VA-Medium	FPC Duluth, MN-Minimum FCI Englewood, CO-Low FCI Florence, CO-Medium SCP Florence, CO-Minimum SCP Greenville, IL-Minimum (F) SCP Leavenworth, KS-Minimum USP Leavenworth, KS-Medium USP Marion, IL-Medium FCI Milan, MI-Low FCI Oxford, WI-Medium SCP Pekin, IL-Minimum FCI Sandstone, MN-Low USMCFP Springfield, MO-Adm. (D) FCI Terre Haute, IN-Medium FCI Waseca, MN-Low (F) FPC Yankton, SD-Minimum (2)	FCI Allenwood, PA-Low FCI Allenwood, PA-Medium FCI Berlin, NH-Medium USP Canaan, PA-High FCI Danbury, CT-Low FSL Danbury, CT-Low (F) (Activating) FCI Elkton, OH-Low FCI Fairton, NJ-Medium FCI Fort Dix, NJ-Low (2) SCP Lewisburg, PA-Minimum SCP McKean, PA-Minimum FCI Schuylkill, PA-Medium
	South Central Region	**Southeast Region**	**Western Region**
	FCI Bastrop, TX-Low FCI Beaumont, TX-Low FCI Beaumont, TX-Medium SCP Beaumont, TX-Minimum USP Beaumont, TX-High FPC Bryan, TX-Minimum (F) FMC Carswell, TX-Adm. (F, D) FMC Carswell, TX-Adm. (F, S) FCI El Reno, OK-Medium FCI Forrest City, AR-Low FCI Forrest City, AR-Medium FMC Fort Worth, TX-Low FCI La Tuna, TX-Low FCI Seagoville, TX-Low (2) SCP Texarkana, TX-Minimum	FCI Coleman, FL-Low USP Coleman, FL-High SCP Edgefield, SC-Minimum FCI Jesup, GA-Medium FCI Marianna, FL-Medium SCP Miami, FL-Minimum FCI Miami, FL-Low (S, 2) FPC Montgomery, AL-Minimum (2) FPC Pensacola, FL-Minimum SCP Talladega, AL- Minimum FCI Tallahassee, FL-Low (F) FCI Yazoo City, MS-Low	FCI Dublin, CA-Low (2, F) FCI Herlong, CA-Medium FCI Lompoc, CA-Low FCI Phoenix, AZ-Medium SCP Phoenix, AZ-Minimum (F) FCI Safford, AZ-Low FCI Sheridan, OR-Medium SCP Sheridan, OR-Minimum (2) FCI Terminal Island, CA – Low FCI Terminal Island, CA – Low (D)
	(D) = Dual Diagnosis Program (F) = Female Program (S) = Spanish Program (2) = 2 Programs at the Facility		

Resolve Program

Program Description	The Resolve Program is a cognitive-behavioral program designed to address the trauma related mental health needs of inmates. Specifically, the program seeks to decrease the incidence of trauma related psychological disorders and improve inmates' level of functioning. In addition, the program aims to increase the effectiveness of other treatments, such as drug treatment and healthcare. The program uses a standardized treatment protocol consisting of three components: an initial psycho-educational workshop (Trauma in Life); a brief, skills based treatment group (Seeking Safety); and Dialectical Behavioral Therapy (DBT), Cognitive Processing Therapy (CPT), and/or a Skills Maintenance Group which are intensive, cognitive-behavioral treatment groups to address persistent psychological and interpersonal difficulties. The Resolve Program is currently available in many female institutions and a limited number of male institutions.
Time Frame	In most instances, inmates are expected to participate in the Resolve Program during their first 12 months of incarceration. The full Resolve Program protocol takes approximately 40 weeks to complete; however, scheduling conflicts may extend the length of the program. Inmates also have the option of continuing to participate in the Skills Maintenance Group indefinitely to continue practicing healthy coping skills.
Admission Criteria	The Resolve Program is for inmates with a mental health diagnosis due to trauma. While the Trauma in Life Workshop is the first stage of the Resolve Program, other inmates without a history of trauma may participate in this workshop if institution resources permit.
Program Content	The program content focuses on the development of personal resilience, effective coping skills, emotional self-regulation, and healthy interpersonal relationships. These skills are attained through the use of educational, cognitive, behavioral, and problem-solving focused interventions. The program materials are modified to be gender responsive to male and female populations.
Empirical Support	Empirical support for the interventions utilized in the Resolve Program is well-established. Seeking Safety, CPT, and DBT appear in multiple evidence-based programs (EBP) registries. These protocols are also used in the Veterans Administration, the country's largest provider of trauma-related treatment.
Applicable Policies	5330.11 CN-1 Psychology Treatment Programs

Institution Locations	The Resolve Program is available at the following facilities:		
	Mid-Atlantic Region	**North Central Region**	**Northeast Region**
	FPC Alderson, WV-Minimum (F)	ADX Florence, CO-Maximum (M)	FCI Danbury, CT-Low (M)
	SFF Hazelton, WV-Low (F)	SCP Greenville, IL-Minimum (F)	SCP Danbury, CT-Minimum (F)
	SCP Lexington, KY-Minimum (F)	FCI Waseca, MN-Low (F)	FSL Danbury, CT-Low (F) (Activating)
	South Central Region	**Southeast Region**	**Western Region**
	FPC Bryan, TX-Minimum (F)	FCI Aliceville, AL-Low (F)	FCI Dublin, CA-Low (F)
	FMC Carswell, TX-Adm. (F)	SCP Coleman, FL-Minimum (F)	SCP Victorville, CA-Minimum (F)
		SCP Marianna, FL-Minimum (F)	
		FCI Tallahassee, FL-Low (F)	
	(F) Female Program (M) = Male Program		

Sex Offender Treatment Program - Nonresidential

Program Description	The Sex Offender Treatment Program – Nonresidential (SOTP-NR) is a moderate intensity program designed for low to moderate risk sexual offenders. The program consists of cognitive-behaviorally based psychotherapy groups, totaling 4-6 hours per week.
Time Frame	Inmates are ordinarily placed in the SOTP-NR during the last 36 months of their sentence and, prioritized by release date. The typical duration of the SOTP-NR is 9-12 months.
Admission Criteria	Most participants in the SOTP-NR have a history of a single sex crime; many are first time inmates serving a sentence for an Internet Sex Offense. The program is voluntary. Prior to placement in the SOTP-NR, prospective participants are screened with a risk assessment instrument to ensure their offense history is commensurate with moderate intensity treatment.
Program Content	The SOTP-NR is designed to target dynamic risk factors associated with re-offense in sex offenders, as demonstrated by empirical research. These factors include: sexual self-regulation deficits and sexual deviancy; criminal thinking and behavior patterns; intimacy skills deficits; and, emotional self-regulation deficits. The program employs cognitive-behavioral techniques, with a primary emphasis on skills acquisition and practice.
Empirical Support	The SOTP-NR is designed to conform to the characteristics of sex offender treatment programs with proven effectiveness in reducing re-offense as demonstrated by outcome research. These characteristics include: 1) stratification of treatment into separate tracks for high and low/ moderate risk inmates; 2) targeting empirically demonstrated dynamic risk factors; and 3) training and oversight to ensure fidelity with the program model.
Applicable Policies	5324.10 Sex Offender Programs

Institution Locations

The SOTP-NR is available at the following facilities:

Mid-Atlantic Region	North Central Region	Northeast Region
FCI Petersburg, VA-Medium	FCI Englewood, CO-Low USP Marion, IL-Medium	FCI Elkton, OH-Low

South Central Region	Southeast Region	Western Region
FMC Carswell, TX-Adm. (F) FCI Seagoville, TX-Low	FCI Marianna, FL-Medium	USP Tucson, AZ-High

(F) = Female Program

Sex Offender Treatment Program - Residential

Program Description	The Sex Offender Treatment Program - Residential (SOTP-R) is a high intensity program designed for high risk sexual offenders. The program consists of cognitive-behaviorally based psychotherapy groups, totaling 10-12 hours per week, on a residential treatment unit employing a modified therapeutic community model.
Time Frame	Inmates are ordinarily placed in the SOTP-R during the last 36 months of their sentence, prioritized by release date. The typical duration of the SOTP-R is 12-18 months.
Admission Criteria	Participants in the SOTP-R have a history of multiple sex crimes, extensive non-sexual criminal histories, and/or a high level of sexual deviancy or hypersexuality. The program is voluntary. Prior to placement in the SOTP-R, prospective participants are screened with a risk assessment instrument to ensure their offense history is commensurate with high intensity treatment.
Program Content	The SOTP-R is designed to target dynamic risk factors associated with re-offense in sex offenders, as demonstrated by empirical research. These factors include: sexual self-regulation deficits and sexual deviancy; criminal thinking and behavior patterns; intimacy skills deficits; and emotional self-regulation deficits. The program employs cognitive-behavioral techniques, with a primary emphasis on skills acquisition and practice. The modified therapeutic community model is employed to address pro-offending attitudes and values.
Empirical Support	The SOTP-R is designed to conform to the characteristics of sex offender treatment programs with a proven effectiveness in reducing re-offense as demonstrated by outcome research. These characteristics include: 1) stratification of treatment into separate tracks for high and low/moderate risk inmates; 2) targeting empirically demonstrated dynamic risk factors; and 3) training and oversight to ensure fidelity with the program model.
Applicable Policies	5324.10 Sex Offender Programs
Institution Locations	The SOTP-R is available at the following facilities: FMC Devens, MA-Adm. USP Marion, IL-Medium

Skills Program

Program Description	The Skills Program is a residential treatment program designed to improve the institutional adjustment of inmates with intellectual disabilities and social deficiencies. The program uses an integrative model which includes a modified therapeutic community, cognitive-behavioral therapies, and skills training. The goal of the program is to increase the academic achievement and adaptive behavior of cognitively impaired inmates, thereby improving their institutional adjustment and likelihood for successful community reentry.
Time Frame	The Skills Program is conducted over 12-18 months. Participation in the program during the initial phase of an inmate's incarceration is recommended; however, inmates may participate in the program at a later time. Formal programming is facilitated half-days, five days a week with the remaining half-day dedicated to an institution work assignment or receiving tutorial assistance.
Admission Criteria	Inmates with significant functional impairment due to intellectual disabilities, neurological deficits, and/or remarkable social skills deficits are considered for the program. Participants must be appropriate for housing in a low or medium security institution. Inmates must volunteer for the program.
Program Content	The Skills Program operates as a modified therapeutic community and utilizes cognitive-behavioral treatments, cognitive rehabilitation, and skills training. The program employs a multi-disciplinary treatment approach aimed at teaching participants basic educational and social skills. Criminal thinking is addressed through the identification of criminal thinking errors and engagement in pro-social interactions with staff and peers. Program content is designed to promote successful reentry into society at the conclusion of their term of incarceration. Program staff collaborate with community partners to facilitate reentry.
Empirical Support	The cognitive-behavioral, cognitive rehabilitation, skills training, and modified therapeutic community interventions selected for this program have sound empirical support and consistently appear in evidence-based programs (EBPs) registries.
Applicable Policies	5330.11 CN-1 Psychology Treatment Programs
Institution Locations	The Skills Program is available at the following facilities: FCI Coleman, FL-Medium FCI Danbury, CT-Low

Steps Toward Awareness, Growth, and Emotional Strength Program

Program Description	The Steps Toward Awareness, Growth, and Emotional Strength (STAGES) Program is a residential treatment program for inmates with serious mental illnesses and a primary diagnosis of Borderline Personality Disorder. The program uses an integrative model which includes a modified therapeutic community, cognitive behavioral therapies, and skills training. The program is designed to increase the time between disruptive behaviors, foster living within the general population or community setting, and increase pro-social skills.
Time Frame	The STAGES Program is typically conducted over 12-18 months. Inmates may participate in the program at any time during their sentence. Formal programming is facilitated half-days, five days a week with the remaining half-day dedicated to an institution work assignment or other programming.
Admission Criteria	Inmates referred to the STAGES Program have a primary diagnosis of Borderline Personality Disorder and a history of unfavorable institutional adjustment linked to this disorder. Examples of unfavorable institutional adjustment include multiple incident reports, suicide watches, and/or extended placement in restrictive housing. Inmates designated to the STAGES Program must volunteer for treatment and be willing to actively engage in the treatment process. Willingness to engage in the treatment is assessed through a brief course of pre-treatment in which the inmate learns basic skills at the referring institution.
Program Content	The program curriculum is derived from Dialectical Behavior Therapy (DBT) and takes place in a modified therapeutic community. There is also an emphasis on basic cognitive-behavioral skills consistent with other Bureau treatment programs. For example, criminal thinking is addressed through the identification of criminal thinking errors and engagement in pro-social interactions with staff and peers. Program content is designed to prepare inmates for transition to less restrictive prison settings and promote successful reentry into society at the conclusion of their term of incarceration. Program staff collaborate with community partners to facilitate reentry.
Empirical Support	DBT is an evidence-based practice for the treatment of Borderline Personality Disorder, with strong empirical support. In addition, the cognitive-behavioral interventions and modified therapeutic community model employed in the program are well supported in the professional literature. These interventions appear in a number of evidence-based programs (EBPs) registries.
Applicable Policies	5330.11 CN-1 Psychology Treatment Programs
Institution Locations	The STAGES Program is available at the following facilities: USP Florence, CO-High (Secure) FCI Terre Haute, IN-Medium

Life Connections Program

Program Description	The Life Connections Program (LCP) is a residential faith-based program offered to inmates of all faith traditions, including for those who do not hold to a religious preference. This program is available to inmates at low, medium, and high security facilities. The goal of LCP is to provide opportunities for the development and maturation of the participants' commitment to normative values and responsibilities, resulting in overall changed behavior and better institutional adjustments. In addition, the participants receive life skills and practical tools and strategies to assist them in transitioning back to society once released from federal custody.
Time Frame	The LCP is an 18 month program in which participants attend classes and meetings, Monday through Friday afternoons for approximately four hours per day, as well as evening mentoring sessions and seminars. In addition, the participants participate in their respective faith services and chapel programs during the evening and weekend hours.
Admission Criteria	Program admission criteria are as follows: • Low security male inmates within 24 to 36 months of their projected release date. • Medium security male inmates with 24 months or more prior to their projected release date. • High security male inmates with 30 months or more prior to their projected release date. • Low security female inmates with 30 months or more prior to their projected release date. • Must not have a written deportation order. • Must not be on Financial Responsibility Program (FRP) Refuse status. • Must have met English-as-a-Second Language (ESL) and GED obligations. • Must receive recommendation from relevant staff (Chaplain, Unit Team, and Associate Warden) and approval from the Warden.
Program Content	The objectives of the program are to foster personal growth and responsibility, and to right the relationships among their victim(s), community, and inmate, using secular outcome-based objectives. The program facilitates the practice of one's personal belief system, whether secular or religious, to bring reconciliation and restoration, and to take responsibility for their criminal behavior. In addition, community organizations and volunteers at the inmates' release destinations serve as mentors to assist and support the participants upon their release.
Empirical Support	The LCP materials and workbooks are based on interactive journaling which was listed on SAMHSA's National Registry of Evidence-based Programs and Practices (NREPP).
Applicable Policies	Operations Memorandum 003-2013 Life Connections Program

The LCP is available at the following facilities:

Mid-Atlantic Region	North Central Region	South Centra Region
FCI Petersburg, VA-Low	USP Leavenworth, KS-Medium FCI Milan, MI-Low USP Terre Haute, IN-High	FMC Carswell, TX-Adm. (F)
(F) = Female Program		

Institution Locations